Can an Aardvark Learn to Bark?

Copyright ©2025 Mark Huenemann
All right reserved.
ISBN – 978-0-9996962-6-2

For my grandchildren

Do you like animals?

Do you like animals that live on a farm?

Do you like animals that live in a zoo?

Do you like animals that live in the jungle? Or the ocean?

Animals can do things that people can't do.

But people can do things animals can't do.

What if animals could do the things that people do?

If you have wondered about that, you are not the only one.

Once, three boys wondered what would happen if animals could do people things.

They asked a lot of questions.

Their questions are in this book.

I hope you enjoy their questions and the pictures of animals doing people things.

If you don't understand something, maybe a grown-up can help.

Their questions begin on the next page.

Have fun reading them!

Can an aardvark learn to bark?

What if ants wore pants?

Does an ape use Scotch tape?

Can a baboon play a tune?

Could a bear dye its hair?

Can a beaver have a fever?

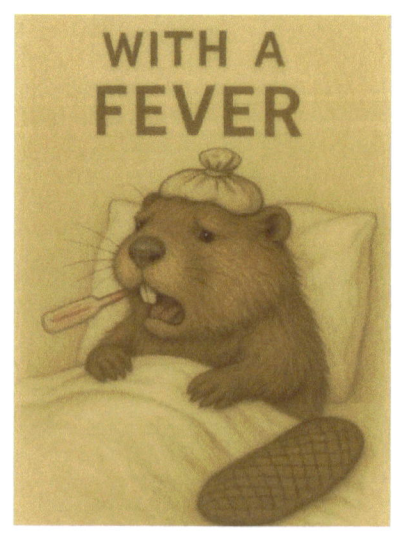

Do bees eat peas?

Can a beetle use a needle?

Can a bird join a herd?

Will a bison use a Dyson?

Did a boa go with Noah?

Can a boar roar?

Will a bobcat wear a hat?

Should you give a bug a hug?

Can a bull get too full?

Will a butterfly eat apple pie?

Does a calf laugh?

Can a camel use enamel?

Would a cat sit in a vat?

Will cattle tattle?

What makes a chicken sicken?

Would a chinchilla live in a villa?

Could a chipmunk flunk?

Is a collie always jolly?

Can a cow pull a plow?

May a coyote own a boat?

Can a crab work in a lab?

What if a crane drove a train?

Will a crocodile run a mile?

Can a crow mow?

Can a deer shift a gear?

Can a dog see in the fog?

Will a duck play in muck?

Is an eagle ever illegal?

Could an eel change a wheel?

Can an egret play a clarinet?

Could an elephant bunt?

Will a fawn fix a lawn?

Does a fish make a wish?

Could a flamingo play bingo?

Will a fly wear a tie?

Could you mail a fox in a box?

Can a frog lift a log?

Should a gator be a hater?

Can a gazelle sell?

What if a giraffe were just half?

Can a gnu be blue?

Can a goat sail a boat?

Can a goose take something loose?

Is a gopher ever a loafer?

Does a gorilla like vanilla?

Can a hawk apply caulk?

Would a hare enjoy the fair?

Can a hen be ten?

Is there a heron named Karen?

Can a hornet play a cornet?

Does a horse have great force?

Is there a hyena named Gina?

Would an iguana like a sauna?

Can a jackal make a tackle?

Should a jaguar drive a car?

Can a jellyfish cook a dish?

Do kangaroos like zoos?

Would a koala like Ocala?

Is there a lamb named Sam?

Have you seen a peppered leopard

Should a lion be fryin'?

Will a lizard eat a Blizzard?

Does a llama miss its mama?

Can a lobster be a mobster?

Does a macaw know how to draw?

Can a mare go up a stair?

Do mink really think?

What if a mole stole?

Would a mongoose like fruit juice?

Does a monkey like chunky?

Should a moose ride in a caboose?

Will a mosquito eat a taquito?

Can a mouse build a house?

Will a mule fill fuel?

Can a narwhal play ball?

Have you seen an ostrich pitch?

Does an otter like food hotter?

Does an owl use a towel?

Do oxen like boxin?

Does an oyster like moisture?

Would you name a panda Amanda?

Will a panther know the answer?

Will a parrot eat a carrot?

Does a pheasant look pleasant?

Will a pig eat a fig?

Should you give a puppy a guppy?

Can a python say "Goodbye son"?

Can a quail pound a nail?

Do rabbits have bad habits?

Will a raccoon stare at the moon?

Can a rat swing a bat?

Can a reindeer feel fear?

Is there an albino rhino?

Does a rooster need a booster?

Do salmon play backgammon?

Can a seal deal?

Should a shark be in the park?

How high can sheep leap?

Why is a skunk in the trunk?

Can a snail read the mail?

Can a snake bake a cake?

Will a sow take a bow?

Can a sparrow shoot an arrow?

Can a spider be a fighter?

Should a stallion wear a medallion?

Does a steer cry a tear?

Can a stork eat with a fork?

Will a tiger eat Braunschweiger?

Can a toad carry a load?

Does a turkey eat jerky?

Can a turtle wear a girdle?

Should a viper wear a diaper?

Can a vole climb a pole?

Could a weasel use an easel?

Will a whale drink from a pail?

Would a wildebeest eat a feast?

Can a wolf play golf?

Would a wombat go to combat?

What makes a worm squirm?

Can a xerus hear us?

Will a yak attack?

Can a zebu see you?

The boys who asked the questions in this book hope you enjoyed them!

And they hope you will think of your own questions about animals.

Thank you for reading this book!

www.ingramcontent.com/pod-product-compliance
Lightning Source LLC
LaVergne TN
LVHW071026070426
835507LV00002B/47